To ....

From ....

PROMISES

FOR A

WOMAN

of Worth

**CHRISTIAN ART
PUBLISHERS**

Promises for a Woman of Worth

Previously published under the title
Becoming a Woman of Worth Promise Book

Copyright © 2015 by Christian Art Publishers
PO Box 1599, Vereeniging, 1930, RSA

Designed by Christian Art Publishers
Compiled by Mairi-Ann Bonnet

Images used under license by Shutterstock.com

Printed in China

ISBN 978-1-4321-1125-0

15 16 17 18 19 20 21 22 23 24 – 12 11 10 9 8 7 6 5 4 3

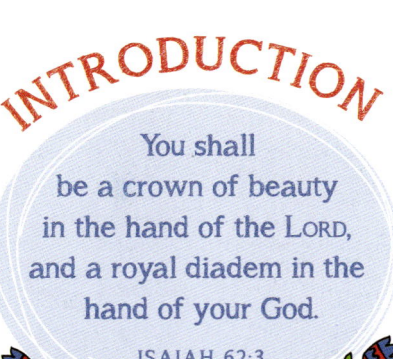

INTRODUCTION

You shall
be a crown of beauty
in the hand of the LORD,
and a royal diadem in the
hand of your God.

ISAIAH 62:3

Do you know that you are a woman of great worth? God designed you with a special purpose and plan. To God you are more precious than rubies and the Scripture verses in this book will help you to live as the rare jewel that you are in the Father's royal diadem. You will find encouragement and inspiration as you strive to shine and reflect the Father's love and light to all around you.

May God's richest blessings be upon you as you seek to become the woman God wants you to be.

CONTENTS

CONTENTS

YOU ARE
WORTH
far more
THAN
RUBIES

PROVERBS 31:10

You are meant to be a woman of **W**-O-R-T-H.
You were designed to walk in God's ways and wait
on Him in faith. He desires your worship and will
make you wise if you just ask Him.

WAITING ON THE LORD

Let God take the initiative. If you will wait, God will work! Cease from your trying; start to trust and praise Him for what He is going to do.

ROBERT D. FOSTER

Live in such a way that God's love can bless you as you wait for the eternal life that our Lord Jesus Christ in His mercy is going to give you.

JUDE 21 NLT

Those who hope in the LORD will renew their strength. They will soar on wings like eagles; they will run and not grow weary, they will walk and not be faint.

ISAIAH 40:31

What I do, God, is wait for You,
wait for my Lord, my God –
You will answer!

PSALM 38:15 THE MESSAGE

We have come to share in Christ
if we hold firmly till the end
the confidence we had at first.

HEBREWS 3:14

Wait for the LORD and keep His way.
He will exalt you to inherit the land.

PSALM 37:34

No one has heard, no ear has perceived,
no eye has seen any God besides You,
who acts on behalf of those who wait for Him.

ISAIAH 64:4

Our soul waits for the LORD;
He is our help and our shield.

PSALM 33:20 NKJV

WALKING IN GOD'S WAYS

The strength and happiness of an individual consists in finding out the way in which God is going, and going that way too.

HENRY WARD BEECHER

Walk in all the way that the LORD your God has commanded you, so that you may live and prosper and prolong your days in the land that you will possess.

DEUTERONOMY 5:33

The LORD will establish you as a holy people to Himself, just as He has sworn to you, if you keep the commandments of the LORD your God and walk in His ways.

DEUTERONOMY 28:9 NKJV

"If you walk in My ways, to keep
My statutes and My commandments,
then I will lengthen your days."

1 KINGS 3:14 NKJV

Those who walk uprightly
enter into peace; they find rest.

ISAIAH 57:2

If we walk in the light, as He is
in the light, we have fellowship
with one another, and the
blood of Jesus, His Son,
purifies us from all sin.

1 JOHN 1:7

"Stand in the ways and see,
and ask for the old paths,
where the good way is, and walk in it;
then you will find rest for your souls."

JEREMIAH 6:16 NKJV

WATCHFUL

**People see
God every day,
they just don't
recognize Him.**

PEARL BAILEY

I watch in hope for the LORD,
I wait for God my Savior;
my God will hear me.

MICAH 7:7

The LORD watches over
all who love Him.

PSALM 145:20

She watches over the affairs
of her household. A woman who
fears the Lord is to be praised.
Give her the reward she has earned,
and let her works bring her praise.

PROVERBS 31:27, 30-31

Be careful!
Watch out for attacks from
the devil, your great enemy.
He prowls around like a roaring lion,
looking for some victim to devour.

1 PETER 5:8 NLT

"I will instruct you and
teach you in the way you should go;
I will counsel you and watch over you."

PSALM 32:8

WEALTH

Life begets life.
Energy begets energy.
It is by spending oneself
that one becomes rich.

SARAH BERNHARDT

Remember the LORD your God, for it is He who gives you the ability to produce wealth, and so confirms His covenant, which He swore to your forefathers, as it is today.

DEUTERONOMY 8:18

"Don't store up treasures here on earth, where they can be eaten by moths and get rusty, and where thieves break in and steal. Store your treasures in heaven, where they will never become moth-eaten or rusty and where they will be safe from thieves."

MATTHEW 6:19-20 NLT

Day by day the LORD takes care
of the innocent, and they will receive
a reward that lasts forever. They
will survive through hard times;
even in famine they will have
more than enough.

PSALM 37:18-19 NLT

Honor the LORD with your wealth
and with the best part of everything
your land produces. Then He will fill
your barns with grain, and your vats
will overflow with the finest wine.

PROVERBS 3:9-10 NLT

Tell those rich in this world's wealth
to quit being so full of themselves
and so obsessed with money. Tell them
to go after God, who piles on all the riches
we could ever manage – to do good,
to be rich in helping others,
to be extravagantly generous.

1 TIMOTHY 6:17-18 THE MESSAGE

WHOLEHEARTED

Jesus gave His
all for me. How can
I give Him less?

ANONYMOUS

Trust in the LORD with all your heart
and lean not on your own understanding;
in all your ways acknowledge Him,
and He will make your paths straight.

PROVERBS 3:5-6

Whatever you do,
work at it with all your heart,
as working for the Lord, not for men.

COLOSSIANS 3:23

But if from there you seek
the Lord your God, you will find
Him if you look for Him with all
your heart and with all your soul.

DEUTERONOMY 4:29

Take your everyday, ordinary life –
your sleeping, eating, going-to-work,
and walking-around life – and place
it before God as an offering.
Embracing what God does for you
is the best thing you can do for Him.

ROMANS 12:1 THE MESSAGE

"Whom shall I send, and who
will go for us?" Then I said,
"Here am I! Send me."

ISAIAH 6:8 NKJV

WILLING TO BE OF SERVICE

Life is an
exciting business,
and it is most exciting
when it is lived for others.

HELEN KELLER

"If you try to keep your life for yourself,
you will lose it. But if you give up your life
for Me, you will find true life."

MATTHEW 16:25 NLT

Serve wholeheartedly, as if you were
serving the Lord, not men, because you know
that the Lord will reward everyone
for whatever good he does.

EPHESIANS 6:7-8

Fear the LORD, and serve Him in truth with all your heart; for consider what great things He has done for you.

1 SAMUEL 12:24 NKJV

Those who have served well gain an excellent standing and great assurance in their faith in Christ Jesus.

1 TIMOTHY 3:13

"Whoever wants to be great must become a servant. Whoever wants to be first among you must be your slave. This is what the Son of Man has done: He came to serve, not be served."

MATTHEW 20:26-28 THE MESSAGE

"My Father will honor the one who serves Me."

JOHN 12:26

WINNING

We have all
eternity to tell of victories
won for Christ, but we have
only a few hours before sunset
in which to win them.

JONATHAN GOFORTH

I press on toward the goal
to win the prize for which God
has called me heavenward
in Christ Jesus.

PHILIPPIANS 3:14

Despite all these things,
overwhelming victory is ours
through Christ, who loved us.

ROMANS 8:37 NLT

Remember that in a race everyone runs,
but only one person gets the prize.
You also must run in such a way that you
will win. I run straight to the goal with
purpose in every step. I discipline my body
like an athlete, training it to do what
it should. Otherwise, I fear that
after preaching to others I myself
might be disqualified.

1 CORINTHIANS 9:24, 26-27 NLT

How we thank God, who gives
us victory over sin and death through
Jesus Christ our Lord!

1 CORINTHIANS 15:57 NLT

The person who wins out over
the world's ways is simply the one who
believes Jesus is the Son of God.

1 JOHN 5:5 THE MESSAGE

WISDOM

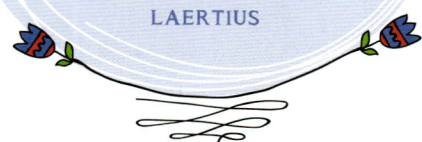

Make wisdom your
provision for the journey
of youth to old age; for it is a
more certain support than all
the other possessions.

LAERTIUS

I keep asking that the God of our
Lord Jesus Christ, the glorious Father,
may give you the Spirit of wisdom and
revelation, so that you may know Him better.

EPHESIANS 1:17

If you need wisdom – if you want to know
what God wants you to do – ask Him,
and He will gladly tell you.

JAMES 1:5 NLT

Wisdom is sweet to your soul;
if you find it, there is a future hope for you,
and your hope will not be cut off.

PROVERBS 24:14

God gives wisdom, knowledge, and joy to
those who please Him.

ECCLESIASTES 2:26 NLT

Wisdom is a good thing and
benefits those who see the sun.
Wisdom preserves the life of its possessor.

ECCLESIASTES 7:11-12

"I will give you words and wisdom
that none of your adversaries will
be able to resist or contradict."

LUKE 21:15

You're blessed when you meet Lady Wisdom,
when you make friends with Madame Insight.

PROVERBS 3:13 THE MESSAGE

WITNESS

To make a
difference in the world,
let Jesus make
a difference in you.

ANONYMOUS

We are Christ's ambassadors, and God
is using us to speak to you. We urge you,
as though Christ Himself were here
pleading with you, "Be reconciled to God!"

2 CORINTHIANS 5:20 NLT

Then Jesus came to them and said, "Go and
make disciples of all nations, baptizing them
in the name of the Father and of the Son and
of the Holy Spirit, and teaching them to obey
everything I have commanded you."

MATTHEW 28:18-20

"If anyone acknowledges Me
publicly here on earth, I, the Son of Man,
will openly acknowledge that person
in the presence of God's angels."

LUKE 12:8 NLT

"Go into all the world and preach
the good news to all creation. Whoever
believes and is baptized will be saved."

MARK 16:15-16

How then shall they call on Him in
whom they have not believed? And how shall
they believe in Him of whom they have not
heard? And how shall they hear without a
preacher? And how shall they preach unless
they are sent? As it is written:
"How beautiful are the feet of those
who preach the gospel of peace,
who bring glad tidings of good things!"

ROMANS 10:14-15 NKJV

WOMANHOOD

**Next to God
we are indebted to
women, first for life itself,
and then for making it
worth having.**

CHRISTIAN BOVEÉ

A kindhearted
woman gains respect.

PROVERBS 11:16

And now, my daughter, don't be afraid.
I will do for you all you ask.
All my fellow townsmen know that
you are a woman of noble character.

RUTH 3:11

She is clothed with strength
and dignity, and she laughs with
no fear of the future. When she speaks,
her words are wise, and kindness is
the rule when she gives instructions.

PROVERBS 31:25-26 NLT

And the LORD God said,
"It is not good for the man to be alone.
I will make a companion who will help him."

GENESIS 2:18 NLT

Beauty should not come from
outward adornment. Instead, it should
be that of your inner self, the unfading
beauty of a gentle and quiet spirit,
which is of great worth in God's sight.

1 PETER 3:3-4

WORK

It is good to dream,
but it is better to dream
and work. Faith is mighty,
but action with faith is mightier.
Desiring is helpful, but work
and desire are invincible.

THOMAS ROBERT GAIN

Commit to the Lord whatever you do,
and your plans will succeed.

PROVERBS 16:3

Hard work always pays off; mere talk
puts no bread on the table.

PROVERBS 14:23 THE MESSAGE

The hand of the diligent will rule.

PROVERBS 12:24 NKJV

Be strong and steady,
always enthusiastic about
the Lord's work, for you know
that nothing you do for the
Lord is ever useless.

1 CORINTHIANS 15:58 NLT

We always thank God for all of you,
mentioning you in our prayers.
We continually remember before
our God and Father your work
produced by faith, your labor
prompted by love, and your
endurance inspired by hope
in our Lord Jesus Christ.

1 THESSALONIANS 1:2-3

You will enjoy the fruit of your labor.
How happy you will be! How rich your life!

PSALM 128:2 NLT

WORSHIP

God is not moved
or impressed with our
worship until our hearts
are moved and
impressed by Him.

KELLY SPARKS

Since we are receiving a kingdom that cannot
be shaken, let us be thankful, and so worship
God acceptably with reverence and awe.

HEBREWS 12:28

What a beautiful thing, God,
to give thanks, to sing an anthem to You,
the High God! To announce Your love each
daybreak, sing Your faithful presence
all through the night.

PSALM 92:1-2 THE MESSAGE

Worship the LORD your God;
it is He who will deliver you from
the hand of all your enemies.

2 KINGS 17:39

Worship the LORD with gladness;
come before Him with joyful songs.

PSALM 100:2

Great is the LORD! He is most worthy of praise!
He is to be revered above all the gods.

PSALM 96:4 NLT

Rejoice in the Lord always. Again I will say,
rejoice! Let your gentleness be known
to all men. The Lord is at hand. Be anxious
for nothing, but in everything by prayer and
supplication, with thanksgiving, let your
requests be made known to God;
and the peace of God, which surpasses
all understanding, will guard your hearts
and minds through Christ Jesus.

PHILIPPIANS 4:4-7 NKJV

WORTHY

The love of God is like the Amazon River flowing down to water one daisy.

ANONYMOUS

Behold what manner of love the Father has bestowed on us, that we should be called children of God!

1 JOHN 3:1 NKJV

I praise You because I am fearfully and wonderfully made; Your works are wonderful, I know that full well.

PSALM 139:14

We are God's masterpiece.

EPHESIANS 2:10 NLT

You are a chosen generation, a royal priesthood, a holy nation, His own special people, that you may proclaim the praises of Him who called you out of darkness into His marvelous light.

1 PETER 2:9 NKJV

"Before I formed you in the womb I knew you, before you were born I set you apart."

JEREMIAH 1:5

"For I know the plans I have for you," declares the LORD, "plans to prosper you and not to harm you, plans to give you hope and a future."

JEREMIAH 29:11

We are transfigured much like the Messiah, our lives gradually becoming brighter and more beautiful as God enters our lives and we become like Him.

2 CORINTHIANS 3:18 THE MESSAGE

You will be blessed
if you obey the commands
of the Lᴏʀᴅ your God that I am
giving you today.

DEUTERONOMY 11:27 NLT

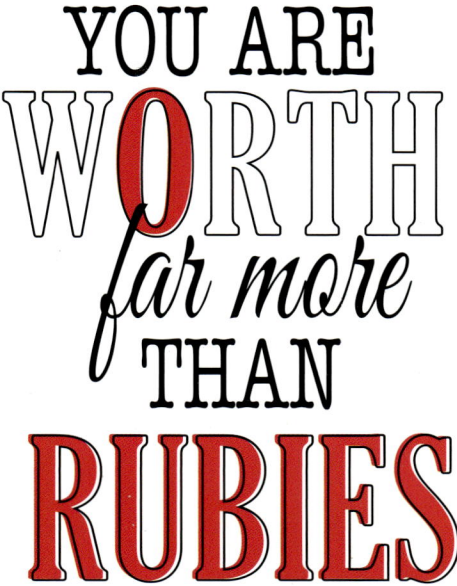

YOU ARE
W**O**RTH
far more
THAN
RUBIES

PROVERBS 31:10

Being a woman of W-**O**-R-T-H means you are open to
God's leading and obedient in serving Him. Knowing that
you are a ruby of great value in God's sight makes you
optimistic and able to overcome obstacles.

OBEDIENCE

Obedience is the means
whereby we show the
earnestness of our desire
to do God's will.

OSWALD CHAMBERS

"Obey Me, and I will be
your God and you will be My people.
Walk in all the ways I command you,
that it may go well with you."

JEREMIAH 7:23

If anyone obeys His word,
God's love is truly made complete in Him.

1 JOHN 2:5

"If you love Me, show it by doing what I've told you. The person who knows My commandments and keeps them, that's who loves Me. And the person who loves Me will be loved by My Father, and I will love him and make Myself plain to him."

JOHN 14:15, 21 THE MESSAGE

"If you walk in My ways, to keep My statutes and My commandments, as your father David walked, then I will lengthen your days."

1 KINGS 3:14 NKJV

"Not everyone who says to Me, 'Lord, Lord,' will enter the kingdom of heaven, but only he who does the will of My Father who is in heaven."

MATTHEW 7:21

OBJECTIVES

Grant that I may
always desire and will
that which is most acceptable
and pleasing to You.

THOMAS À KEMPIS

I keep working toward that day
when I will finally be all that Christ Jesus
saved me for and wants me to be. I strain
to reach the end of the race and receive
the prize for which God, through
Christ Jesus, is calling us up to heaven.

PHILIPPIANS 3:12, 14 NLT

You ought to say, "If it is the Lord's will,
we will live and do this or that."

JAMES 4:15

I eagerly expect and hope that I
will in no way be ashamed, but will have
sufficient courage so that now as always
Christ will be exalted in my body,
whether by life or by death. For to me,
to live is Christ and to die is gain.

PHILIPPIANS 1:20-21

Everything else is worthless when
compared with the priceless gain of
knowing Christ Jesus my Lord. I have
discarded everything else, counting
it all as garbage, so that I may have
Christ and become one with Him.

PHILIPPIANS 3:8-9 NLT

"I have raised you up for this
very purpose, that I might show you
My power and that My name might be
proclaimed in all the earth."

EXODUS 9:16

OBSERVANT

To acquire knowledge,
one must study;
but to acquire wisdom,
one must observe.

MARILYN VOS SAVANT

Consider the blameless,
observe the upright; there is a future
for the man of peace.

PSALM 37:37

I took a long look and pondered
what I saw; the fields preached
me a sermon and I listened.

PROVERBS 24:32 THE MESSAGE

My Strength, I watch for You;
You, O God, are my fortress,
my loving God.
God will go before me.

PSALM 59:9-10

Happy are those who listen to me,
watching for me daily at my gates,
waiting for me outside my home!
For whoever finds me finds life
and wins approval from the LORD.
But those who miss me have
injured themselves.

PROVERBS 8:34-36 NLT

Watch out that you do not
lose what you have worked for,
but that you may be rewarded fully.

2 JOHN 8

OFFERINGS

You can give
without loving,
but you cannot love
without giving.

AMY CARMICHAEL

Let each one give as he purposes in his heart,
not grudgingly or of necessity;
for God loves a cheerful giver.

2 CORINTHIANS 9:7 NKJV

May He remember all your sacrifices and
accept your burnt offerings. May He give you
the desire of your heart and make all your
plans succeed.

PSALM 20:3-4

"This poor widow has given more
than all the rest of them.
For they have given a tiny part
of their surplus, but she, poor as she is,
has given everything she has."

LUKE 21:3-4 NLT

"Bring your full tithe to the Temple
treasury so there will be ample provisions
in My Temple. Test Me in this and see if I don't
open up heaven itself to you and pour out
blessings beyond your wildest dreams."

MALACHI 3:10 THE MESSAGE

Offer your bodies as living sacrifices,
holy and pleasing to God. Do not conform
any longer to the pattern of this world, but be
transformed by the renewing of your mind.
Then you will be able to test and approve
what God's will is – His good,
pleasing and perfect will.

ROMANS 12:1-2

OFFSPRING

If you want your
child to walk the righteous
path, do not merely point
the way – lead the way.

J. A. ROSENKRANZ

He put a child in the middle of the room.
Then, cradling the little one in His arms,
He said, "Whoever embraces one of these
children as I do embraces Me, and far
more than Me – God who sent Me."

MARK 9:36-37 THE MESSAGE

Train up a child in the way he should go,
and when he is old he will not depart from it.

PROVERBS 22:6 NKJV

Who can find a virtuous wife?
For her worth is far above rubies.
Her children rise up and call her blessed;
her husband also, and he praises her.

PROVERBS 31:10, 28 NKJV

Children's children are a crown to the aged,
and parents are the pride of their children.

PROVERBS 17:6

Once I was young, and now I am old.
Yet I have never seen the godly forsaken,
nor seen their children begging for bread.
The godly always give generous loans to
others, and their children are a blessing.

PSALM 37:25-26 NLT

All your children will have God for their
teacher – what a mentor for your children!

ISAIAH 54:13 THE MESSAGE

OPEN-HANDED

The world says,
the more you take,
the more you have.
Christ says,
the more you give,
the more you are.

FREDERICK BUECHNER

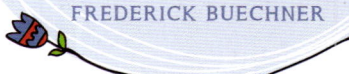

As each one has received a gift,
minister it to one another, as good
stewards of the manifold grace of God.

1 PETER 4:10 NKJV

The good person is generous
and lends lavishly; no shuffling or
stumbling around for this one, but a
sterling and solid and lasting reputation.

PSALM 112:5-6 THE MESSAGE

If you help the poor,
you are lending to the LORD –
and He will repay you!

PROVERBS 19:17 NLT

You will be enriched so that
you can give even more generously.
And when we take your gifts to those
who need them, they will break
out in thanksgiving to God.

2 CORINTHIANS 9:11 NLT

Let them do good, that they be
rich in good works, ready to give,
willing to share, storing up for
themselves a good foundation
for the time to come, that they
may lay hold on eternal life.

1 TIMOTHY 6:18-19 NKJV

OPEN-HEARTED

God is the source
of love; Christ is the
proof of love; service is the
expression of love; boldness
is the outcome of love.

HENRIETTA C. MEARS

Anyone who loves other
Christians is living in the light and
does not cause anyone to stumble.

1 JOHN 2:10 NLT

May the Lord make your love grow and
overflow to each other and to everyone else,
just as our love overflows toward you.

1 THESSALONIANS 3:12 NLT

"Love your enemies, do good to them, and lend to them without expecting to get anything back. Then your reward will be great, and you will be sons of the Most High, because He is kind to the ungrateful and wicked. Be merciful, just as your Father is merciful."

LUKE 6:35-36

Make every effort to add to your faith brotherly kindness; and to brotherly kindness, love. For if you possess these qualities in increasing measure, they will keep you from being ineffective and unproductive in your knowledge of our Lord Jesus Christ.

2 PETER 1:5, 7-8

If we love one another, God dwells deeply within us, and His love becomes complete in us – perfect love!

1 JOHN 4:12 THE MESSAGE

OPTIMISTIC

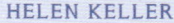

Optimism is the faith that leads to achievement. Nothing can be done without hope and confidence.

HELEN KELLER

A cheerful look brings joy to the heart; good news makes for good health.

PROVERBS 15:30 NLT

I have learned the secret of living in every situation, whether it is with a full stomach or empty, with plenty or little. For I can do everything with the help of Christ who gives me the strength I need.

PHILIPPIANS 4:12-13 NLT

I'm sure now I'll see God's
goodness in the exuberant earth.
Stay with God! Take heart. Don't quit.

PSALM 27:13-14 THE MESSAGE

This is the confidence that we
have in Him, that if we ask anything
according to His will, He hears us.

1 JOHN 5:14 NKJV

Praise be to the God and Father of our Lord
Jesus Christ! In His great mercy He has given
us new birth into a living hope through the
resurrection of Jesus Christ from the dead,
and into an inheritance that can never perish,
spoil or fade – kept in heaven for you.

1 PETER 1:3-4

So we may boldly say, "The LORD is my helper;
I will not fear. What can man do to me?"

HEBREWS 13:6 NKJV

ORGANIZED

**Failing to plan
is knowingly
planning to fail.**

ANONYMOUS

A good woman is hard to find,
and worth far more than diamonds.
She's up before dawn, preparing breakfast for
her family and organizing her day. She looks
over a field and buys it, then, with money
she's put aside, plants a garden.

PROVERBS 31:10, 15-16 THE MESSAGE

Commit your work to the LORD,
and then your plans will succeed.

PROVERBS 16:3 NLT

Good planning and
hard work lead to prosperity,
but hasty shortcuts lead to poverty.

PROVERBS 21:5 NLT

Those who plan what is
good find love and faithfulness.

PROVERBS 14:22

She keeps an eye on everyone
in her household, and keeps them
all busy and productive.

PROVERBS 31:27 THE MESSAGE

The plans of the diligent
lead to profit as surely as
haste leads to poverty.

PROVERBS 21:5

OVERCOMING

**In Christ
we are overcomers.**

ANONYMOUS

We can rejoice when we run into problems
and trials, for we know that they are
good for us – they help us learn to endure.
And endurance develops strength of
character in us, and character strengthens
our confident expectation of salvation.

ROMANS 5:3-4 NLT

Patient endurance leads to godliness.

2 PETER 1:6 NLT

To [everyone] who overcomes, I will give
the right to eat from the tree of life,
which is in the paradise of God.

REVELATION 2:7

Everyone born of God overcomes
the world. This is the victory that has
overcome the world, even our faith.

1 JOHN 5:4

"Conquerors will march in the victory parade,
their names indelible in the Book of Life.
I'll lead them up and present them by
name to My Father and His Angels."

REVELATION 3:5 THE MESSAGE

Do not be overcome by evil,
but overcome evil with good.

ROMANS 12:21

OVERLOOK WRONGS

We evaluate others
with a godlike justice,
but we want them
to evaluate us with a
godlike compassion.

SYDNEY J. HARRIS

Hatred stirs up strife, but love covers all sins.

PROVERBS 10:12 NKJV

"Don't pick on people, jump on their failures,
criticize their faults – unless, of course, you
want the same treatment. It's easy to see
a smudge on your neighbor's face and be
oblivious to the ugly sneer on your own."

MATTHEW 7:1-3 THE MESSAGE

Be kind and compassionate
to one another, forgiving each other,
just as in Christ God forgave you.

EPHESIANS 4:32

Bear with each other and forgive whatever
grievances you may have against one
another. Forgive as the Lord forgave you.

COLOSSIANS 3:13

"If you forgive those who sin against you,
your heavenly Father will forgive you.
But if you refuse to forgive others,
your Father will not forgive your sins."

MATTHEW 6:14-15 NLT

Most important of all, continue to
show deep love for each other,
for love covers a multitude of sins.

1 PETER 4:8 NLT

OWNING UP

We must lay
before Him what is in us,
not what ought to be in us.

C. S. LEWIS

If we confess our sins to Him,
He is faithful and just to forgive us
and to cleanse us from every wrong.

1 JOHN 1:9 NLT

You can't whitewash your sins
and get by with it; you find mercy
by admitting and leaving them.

PROVERBS 28:13 THE MESSAGE

"Come now, let us reason together,"
says the LORD. "Though your sins
are like scarlet, they shall be as
white as snow; though they are red
as crimson, they shall be like wool."

ISAIAH 1:18

When Jesus saw their faith, He said
to the paralytic, "Son, be of good cheer;
your sins are forgiven you."

MATTHEW 9:2 NKJV

What joy for those whose record
the LORD has cleared of sin, whose
lives are lived in complete honesty.

PSALM 32:2 NLT

The ways of right-living
people glow with light;
the longer they live,
the brighter they shine.

PROVERBS 4:18 THE MESSAGE

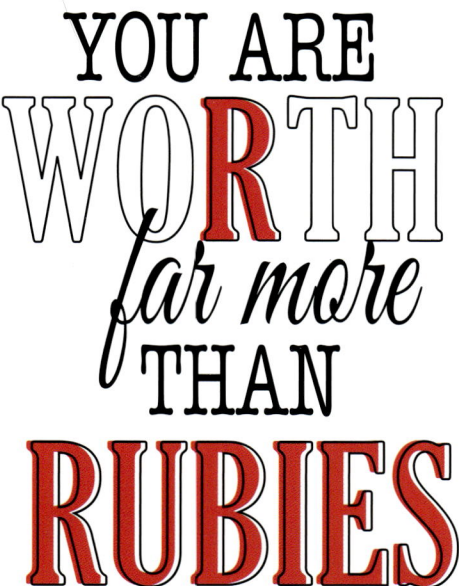

YOU ARE
WORTH
far more
THAN
RUBIES

PROVERBS 31:10

A woman of W-O-**R**-T-H radiates the love of
God and knows she is a rare treasure.
She rejoices in each new day and reaches out
to others to help in any way she can.

RADIANT

The radiance
of the divine beauty is
wholly inexpressible;
words cannot describe it,
nor the ear grasp it.

PHILIMON

You changed wild lament into whirling dance;
You ripped off my black mourning band and
decked me with wildflowers. I'm about to burst
with song; I can't keep quiet about You.

PSALM 30:11-12 THE MESSAGE

Moses was not aware that his face was
radiant because he had spoken with the LORD.

EXODUS 34:29

Blessed are the people who know the passwords of praise, who shout on parade in the bright presence of God. Your vibrant beauty has gotten inside us – you've been so good to us! We're walking on air!

PSALM 89:15, 17 THE MESSAGE

All of us have had that veil removed so that we can be mirrors that brightly reflect the glory of the Lord. And as the Spirit of the Lord works within us, we become more and more like Him and reflect His glory even more.

2 CORINTHIANS 3:18 NLT

Light is shed upon the righteous and joy on the upright in heart.

PSALM 97:11

RARE

**God loves each
of us as if there were
only one of us.**

ST. AUGUSTINE

There's no one like her on earth,
never has been, never will be. She's a woman
beyond compare. My dove is perfection,
pure and innocent as the day she was born,
and cradled in joy by her mother.

SONG OF SONGS 6:8-9 THE MESSAGE

"I will not forget you!
See, I have engraved you
on the palms of My hands."

ISAIAH 49:15-16

You have been set apart
as holy to the LORD your God, and He has
chosen you to be His own special treasure
from all the nations of the earth.

DEUTERONOMY 14:2 NLT

"I paid a huge price for you.
That's how much you mean to me!
That's how much I love you! I'd sell off
the whole world to get you back,
trade the creation just for you."

ISAIAH 43:3-4 THE MESSAGE

"You have seen how I carried
you on eagles' wings and brought you to Me.
If you will listen obediently to what I say
and keep My covenant, out of all peoples
you'll be My special treasure. The whole Earth
is Mine to choose from, but you're special:
a kingdom of priests, a holy nation."

EXODUS 19:4-6 THE MESSAGE

REACHING OUT

We are all pencils
in the hand of a writing
God, who is sending love
letters to the world.

MOTHER TERESA

"Love your enemies! Do good to them! Lend to
them! And don't be concerned that they might
not repay. Then your reward from heaven will
be very great, and you will truly be acting as
children of the Most High."

LUKE 6:35 NLT

"'Love the Lord your God with all your heart
and with all your soul and with all your
strength and with all your mind,'
and, 'love your neighbor as yourself.'"

LUKE 10:27

If you see some brother or sister in need and have the means to do something about it but turn a cold shoulder and do nothing, what happens to God's love? It disappears. And you made it disappear.

1 JOHN 3:17-18 THE MESSAGE

Suppose a brother or sister is without clothes and daily food. If one of you says to him, "Go, I wish you well; keep warm and well fed," but does nothing about his physical needs, what good is it? In the same way, faith by itself, if it is not accompanied by action, is dead.

JAMES 2:15-17

"'When did we see You a stranger and take You in, or naked and clothe You?' And the King will answer and say to them, 'Assuredly, I say to you, inasmuch as you did it to one of the least of these My brethren, you did it to Me.'"

MATTHEW 25:38, 40 NKJV

REASONABLE

If you make
use of your reason,
you are like one who eats
substantial food; but if you are
moved by the satisfaction of
your will, you are like one
who eats insipid fruit.

JOHN OF THE CROSS

"I will give you a wise and discerning
heart, so that there will never have been
anyone like you, nor will there ever be."

1 KINGS 3:12

The fear of the LORD is the
beginning of wisdom, and the knowledge
of the Holy One is understanding.

PROVERBS 9:10 NKJV

You will keep in perfect
peace all who trust in You,
whose thoughts are fixed on You.

ISAIAH 26:3 NLT

To acquire wisdom
is to love oneself;
people who cherish
understanding will prosper.

PROVERBS 19:8 NLT

Slowness to anger makes for deep
understanding, a quick-tempered
person stockpiles stupidity.

PROVERBS 14:29 THE MESSAGE

People ruin their lives by their
own foolishness and then are
angry at the LORD.

PROVERBS 19:3 NLT

REFLECTIVE

If Jesus crucified
were often in our hearts
and in our memory, we should
soon be learned in all things
that are necessary for us.

THOMAS À KEMPIS

I have more understanding
than all my teachers, for Your
testimonies are my meditation.

PSALM 119:99 NKJV

Reflect on what I am saying,
for the Lord will give you insight
into all of this.

2 TIMOTHY 2:7

Fix your thoughts on Jesus, the Apostle
and High Priest whom we confess.

HEBREWS 3:1

I took all this in and thought it through,
inside and out. Here's what I understood:
The good, the wise, and all that they
do are in God's hands.

ECCLESIASTES 9:1 THE MESSAGE

Fix your thoughts on what is
true and honorable and right.
Think about things that are pure and
lovely and admirable. Think about things
that are excellent and worthy of praise.

PHILIPPIANS 4:8 NLT

I remember the days of old.
I ponder all Your great works.
I think about what You have done.

PSALM 143:5 NLT

REJOICING

**This day and
your life are God's gift
to you – so give thanks
and be joyful always!**

JIM BEGGS

That day they offered great sacrifices,
an exuberant celebration because
God had filled them with great joy.

NEHEMIAH 12:43 THE MESSAGE

Let all who take refuge in You be glad;
let them ever sing for joy. Spread Your
protection over them, that those who love
Your name may rejoice in You. For surely,
O LORD, You bless the righteous; You surround
them with Your favor as with a shield.

PSALM 5:11-12

Rejoice to the extent that
you partake of Christ's sufferings,
that when His glory is revealed,
you may also be glad with exceeding joy.

1 PETER 4:13 NKJV

"Rejoice and be exceedingly glad,
for great is your reward in heaven."

MATTHEW 5:12 NKJV

The godly will rejoice in the LORD
and find shelter in Him. And those
who do what is right will praise Him.

PSALM 64:10 NLT

I trust in Your unfailing love.
I will rejoice because You have
rescued me. I will sing to the LORD
because He has been so good to me.

PSALM 13:5-6 NLT

REPENTANT

Repentance
was perhaps best defined
by a small girl: "It's to be
sorry enough to quit."

C. H. KILMER

This is what the Sovereign Lord,
the Holy One of Israel, says: "In repentance
and rest is your salvation, in quietness
and trust is your strength."

ISAIAH 30:15

The Lord is not slow in keeping His promise,
as some understand slowness. He is patient
with you, not wanting anyone to perish, but
everyone to come to repentance.

2 PETER 3:9

God can use sorrow in our lives to help us turn away from sin and seek salvation. We will never regret that kind of sorrow.

2 CORINTHIANS 7:10 NLT

"If you return to Me, I will restore you so you can continue to serve Me."

JEREMIAH 15:19 NLT

If we confess our sins, He is faithful and just to forgive us our sins and to cleanse us from all unrighteousness.

1 JOHN 1:9 NKJV

"I say to you, there is joy in the presence of the angels of God over one sinner who repents."

LUKE 15:10 NKJV

Now it's time to change your ways! Turn to face God so He can wipe away your sins, pour out showers of blessing to refresh you.

ACTS 3:19 THE MESSAGE

RESPECTFUL

Without respect,
love cannot go far or
rise high: it is an angel
with but one wing.

ALEXANDRE DUMAS

"My covenant was with him, a covenant
of life and peace, and I gave them to him;
this called for reverence and he revered Me
and stood in awe of My name."

MALACHI 2:5

Love each other with genuine affection,
and take delight in honoring each other.

ROMANS 12:10 NLT

A kindhearted woman gains respect.

PROVERBS 11:16

Do you see what we've got?
An unshakable Kingdom!
And do you see how thankful
we must be? Not only thankful,
but brimming with worship,
deeply reverent before God.

HEBREWS 12:28 THE MESSAGE

Ask yourself what you
want people to do for you,
then grab the initiative
and do it for them.

MATTHEW 7:12 THE MESSAGE

"Show your fear of God by
standing up in the presence of
elderly people and showing respect
for the aged. I am the LORD."

LEVITICUS 19:32 NLT

RESPONSIBLE

Character – the willingness to accept responsibility for one's own life – is the source from which self-respect springs.

JOAN DIDION

If God has given you leadership ability, take the responsibility seriously.

ROMANS 12:8 NLT

"To those who use well what they are given, even more will be given, and they will have an abundance."

MATTHEW 25:29 NLT

Obey your leaders and submit
to their authority. They keep watch
over you as men who must give
an account. Obey them so that
their work will be a joy,
not a burden, for that would
be of no advantage to you.

HEBREWS 13:17

The wise woman builds her house,
but with her own hands the
foolish one tears hers down.

PROVERBS 14:1

You put us in charge of
Your handcrafted world,
repeated to us Your Genesis-charge,
made us lords of sheep and cattle,
even animals out in the wild.

PSALM 8:6-7 THE MESSAGE

RICH

God is more
anxious to bestow
His blessings on us than
we are to receive them.

ST. AUGUSTINE

Hasn't God chosen the poor
in this world to be rich in faith? Aren't
they the ones who will inherit the kingdom
God promised to those who love Him?

JAMES 2:5 NLT

Happy are those who fear the LORD.
Yes, happy are those who delight in
doing what He commands. They themselves
will be wealthy, and their good deeds
will never be forgotten.

PSALM 112:1, 3 NLT

Committed and persistent work pays off;
get-rich-quick schemes are ripoffs.

PROVERBS 28:20 THE MESSAGE

You will be made rich in every way
so that you can be generous on every
occasion, and through us your generosity
will result in thanksgiving to God.

2 CORINTHIANS 9:11

You are a chosen generation,
a royal priesthood, a holy nation,
His own special people, that you may
proclaim the praises of Him who called you
out of darkness into His marvelous light.

1 PETER 2:9 NKJV

What are mortals that You should think of us,
mere humans that You should care for us?
For You made us only a little lower than God,
and You crowned us with glory and honor.

PSALM 8:4-5 NLT

RIGHTEOUS

God never alters
the robe of righteousness
to fit the man,
but the man to fit the robe.

ANONYMOUS

The righteous cry out, and the LORD hears,
and delivers them out of all their troubles.

PSALM 34:17 NKJV

And now the prize awaits me – the
crown of righteousness that the Lord,
the righteous Judge, will give me on that
great day of His return. And the prize is
not just for me but for all who eagerly
look forward to His glorious return.

2 TIMOTHY 4:8 NLT

The ways of right-living people
glow with light; the longer they live,
the brighter they shine.

PROVERBS 4:18 THE MESSAGE

The eyes of the LORD are on the righteous,
and His ears are open to their prayers.

1 PETER 3:12 NKJV

When the kindness and love of God our
Savior appeared, He saved us, not because of
righteous things we had done, but because of
His mercy. He saved us through the washing
of rebirth and renewal by the Holy Spirit.

TITUS 3:4-5

"The righteous will shine like the
sun in the kingdom of their Father."

MATTHEW 13:43

ROMANTIC

A good marriage is like an incredible retirement fund. You put everything you have into it ... and over the years it turns from silver to gold to platinum.

WILLARD SCOTT

A man shall leave his father and mother and be joined to his wife, and they shall become one flesh.

GENESIS 2:24 NKJV

"My lover is mine, and I am his. He feeds among the lilies! Before the dawn comes and the shadows flee away, come back to me, my love. Run like a gazelle or a young stag on the rugged mountains."

SONG OF SONGS 2:16-17 NLT

Wives, submit to your husbands,
as is fitting in the Lord.
Husbands, love your wives
and do not be harsh with them.

COLOSSIANS 3:18-19

The man who finds a wife finds a
treasure and receives favor from the LORD.

PROVERBS 18:22 NLT

The fire of love stops at nothing – it sweeps
everything before it. Flood waters can't
drown love, torrents of rain can't put it out.
Love can't be bought, love can't be sold –
it's not to be found in the marketplace.

SONG OF SONGS 8:6-7 THE MESSAGE

ROOTED

Faith is the gaze of the soul upon a saving God, a continuous gaze of the heart at the Triune God.

A. W. TOZER

Just as you accepted
Christ Jesus as your Lord,
you must continue to live in
obedience to Him. Let your
roots grow down into
Him and draw up nourishment
from Him, so you will grow in faith,
strong and vigorous in the truth
you were taught.

COLOSSIANS 2:6-7 NLT

Let us fix our eyes on Jesus, the author and perfecter of our faith, who for the joy set before Him endured the cross, scorning its shame, and sat down at the right hand of the throne of God.

HEBREWS 12:2

Blessed are those who trust in the Lord and have made the Lord their hope and confidence. They are like trees planted along a riverbank, with roots that reach deep into the water. Such trees are not bothered by the heat or worried by long months of drought. Their leaves stay green, and they go right on producing delicious fruit.

JEREMIAH 17:7-8 NLT

According to the grace of God which was given to me, as a wise master builder I have laid the foundation, and another builds on it. But let each one take heed how he builds on it. For no other foundation can anyone lay than that which is laid, which is Jesus Christ.

1 CORINTHIANS 3:10-11 NKJV

"I have called you by
your name; you are Mine.
You have been honored,
and I have loved you."

ISAIAH 43:1, 4 NKJV

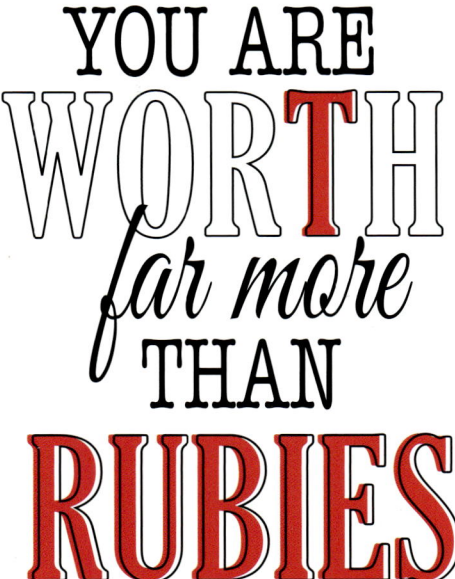

YOU ARE
WORTH
far more
THAN
RUBIES

PROVERBS 31:10

A woman of W-O-R-**T**-H trusts and follows her Teacher.
She is thankful for every lesson learned
along the road she travels with Him.

TACTFUL

Tact is rubbing
out another's
mistake instead
of rubbing it in.

ANONYMOUS

Be of one mind, having compassion for one
another; love as brothers, be tenderhearted,
be courteous; not returning evil for evil or
reviling for reviling, but on the contrary blessing.

1 PETER 3:8-9 NKJV

"For out of the overflow of the heart the
mouth speaks. The good man brings
good things out of the good stored up in him.
For by your words you will be acquitted,
and by your words you will be condemned."

MATTHEW 12:34-35, 37

If you shout a pleasant greeting to
your neighbor too early in the morning,
it will be counted as a curse!

PROVERBS 27:14 NLT

Kind words are like honey – sweet to the soul
and healthy for the body.

PROVERBS 16:24 NLT

Words satisfy the soul as food
satisfies the stomach; the right words
on a person's lips bring satisfaction.

PROVERBS 18:20 NLT

The Master, God, has given me a
well-taught tongue, so I know how
to encourage tired people.

ISAIAH 50:4 THE MESSAGE

Rash language cuts and maims, but there is
healing in the words of the wise.

PROVERBS 12:18 THE MESSAGE

TALENTED

Your talent is
God's gift to you.
What you do with
it is your gift to God.

LEO BUSCAGLIA

Each person is given something
to do that shows who God is: Everyone
gets in on it, everyone benefits. All kinds
of things are handed out by the Spirit,
and to all kinds of people!

1 CORINTHIANS 12:7 THE MESSAGE

Since you are so eager to have
spiritual gifts, ask God for those that
will be of real help to the whole church.

1 CORINTHIANS 14:12 NLT

We have different gifts, according to the grace given us. If a man's gift is prophesying, let him use it in proportion to his faith. If it is serving, let him serve; if it is teaching, let him teach; if it is encouraging, let him encourage; if it is contributing to the needs of others, let him give generously; if it is leadership, let him govern diligently; if it is showing mercy, let him do it cheerfully.

ROMANS 12:6-8

Each one should use whatever gift he has received to serve others, faithfully administering God's grace in its various forms. If anyone speaks, he should do it as one speaking the very words of God. If anyone serves, he should do it with the strength God provides, so that in all things God may be praised through Jesus Christ.

1 PETER 4:10-11

How we praise God, the Father of our Lord Jesus Christ, who has blessed us with every spiritual blessing in the heavenly realms because we belong to Christ.

EPHESIANS 1:3 NLT

TEACHER

You teach a little
by what you say.
You teach most by
what you are.

HENRIETTA C. MEARS

Teach your children to choose
the right path, and when they are older,
they will remain upon it.

PROVERBS 22:6 NLT

"Do not worry about how you will
defend yourselves or what you will say,
for the Holy Spirit will teach you at
that time what you should say."

LUKE 12:11-12

Pay close attention, friend, to what your father tells you; never forget what you learned at your mother's knee. Wear their counsel like flowers in your hair, like rings on your fingers.

PROVERBS 1:8-9 THE MESSAGE

To discipline and reprimand a child produces wisdom, but a mother is disgraced by an undisciplined child.

PROVERBS 29:15 NLT

When she speaks, her words are wise, and kindness is the rule when she gives instructions.

PROVERBS 31:26 NLT

"You will be able to tell wonderful stories to your children and grandchildren about the marvelous things I am doing."

EXODUS 10:2 NLT

TENDER-HEARTED

If I can put one touch
of rosy sunset into
the life of any man or woman,
I shall feel that I have
worked with God.

JOHN MACDONALD

Be kind to each other, tenderhearted,
forgiving one another, just as God through
Christ has forgiven you.

EPHESIANS 4:32 NLT

Your own soul is nourished when
you are kind, but you destroy
yourself when you are cruel.

PROVERBS 11:17 NLT

Do nothing out of selfish ambition or vain conceit, but in humility consider others better than yourselves.

PHILIPPIANS 2:3

"You must be compassionate, just as your Father is compassionate."

LUKE 6:36 NLT

What happens when we live God's way? He brings gifts into our lives, much the same way that fruit appears in an orchard – things like affection for others, exuberance about life, serenity. We develop a sense of compassion in the heart.

GALATIANS 5:22-23 THE MESSAGE

THANKFUL

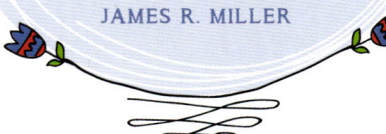

Thanksgiving
is nothing if not a glad
and reverent lifting of the
heart to God in honor and
praise for His goodness.

JAMES R. MILLER

Wealth and honor come from You. In Your
hands are strength and power to exalt and
give strength to all. We give You thanks,
and praise Your glorious name.

1 CHRONICLES 29:12-13

The Lord is my strength, my shield from every
danger. I trust in Him with all my heart.
He helps me, and my heart is filled with joy.
I burst out in songs of thanksgiving.

PSALM 28:7 NLT

I will praise You, for You have answered me,
and have become my salvation.

PSALM 118:21 NKJV

We thank You, O God, Sovereign-Strong,
Who Is and Who Was. You took Your
great power and took over – reigned!

REVELATION 11:17 THE MESSAGE

We ought always to thank God for you,
brothers loved by the Lord, because from
the beginning God chose you to be saved
through the sanctifying work of the Spirit
and through belief in the truth.

2 THESSALONIANS 2:13

Thanks be to God, who gives us the
victory through our Lord Jesus Christ.

1 CORINTHIANS 15:57 NKJV

THOUGHTFUL

Thoughts lead
on to purposes; purposes
go forth in action; actions
form habits; habits decide
character; and character
fixes our destiny.

TRYON EDWARDS

Fix your thoughts on what is true and
honorable and right. Think about things
that are pure and lovely and admirable.
Think about things that are excellent
and worthy of praise.

PHILIPPIANS 4:8 NLT

"You're blessed when you get your inside
world – your mind and heart – put right.
Then you can see God in the outside world."

MATTHEW 5:8 THE MESSAGE

I am so glad, dear friends,
that you always keep me in your
thoughts and you are following the
Christian teaching I passed on to you.

1 CORINTHIANS 11:2 NLT

I have never stopped thanking
God for you. I pray for you constantly.

EPHESIANS 1:16 NLT

"Ask yourself what you want people
to do for you, then grab the initiative
and do it for them."

MATTHEW 7:12 THE MESSAGE

I'm glad in God, far happier than you
would ever guess – happy that you're again
showing such strong concern for me.
Not that you ever quit praying and thinking
about me. It was a beautiful thing that you
came alongside me in my troubles.

PHILIPPIANS 4:10, 14 THE MESSAGE

TOLERANT

Tolerance consists
of seeing certain things
with your heart instead
of with your eyes.

ORLANDO A. BATTISTA

Love is patient and kind.

1 CORINTHIANS 13:4 NLT

A gentle response defuses anger,
but a sharp tongue kindles a temper-fire.

PROVERBS 15:1 THE MESSAGE

"Blessed are the merciful,
for they will be shown mercy."

MATTHEW 5:7

Be agreeable, be sympathetic,
be loving, be compassionate, be humble.
No retaliation. No sharp-tongued sarcasm.
Instead, bless – that's your job, to bless.

1 PETER 3:8-9 THE MESSAGE

Speak and act as those who are going to
be judged by the law that gives freedom,
because judgment without mercy will be
shown to anyone who has not been merciful.
Mercy triumphs over judgment!

JAMES 2:12-13

Cease from anger, and forsake wrath;
do not fret – it only causes harm.

PSALM 37:8 NKJV

Better a patient man than a warrior,
a man who controls his temper
than one who takes a city.

PROVERBS 16:32

TRAVELER

If you are a Christian,
you are not a citizen of this
world trying to get to heaven;
you are a citizen of
heaven making your
way through this world.

VANCE HAVNER

All these faithful ones …
agreed that they were no more than
foreigners and nomads here on earth.
And obviously people who talk like that are
looking forward to a country they can call
their own. If they had meant the country
they came from, they would have found
a way to go back. But they were looking for a
better place, a heavenly homeland. God
has prepared a heavenly city for them.

HEBREWS 11:13-16 NLT

Friends, this world is not your home,
so don't make yourselves cosy in it. Live an
exemplary life among the natives so that
your actions will refute their prejudices.

1 PETER 2:11-12 THE MESSAGE

We're citizens of high heaven! We're waiting
the arrival of the Savior, the Master, Jesus
Christ, who will transform our earthy bodies
into glorious bodies like His own.

PHILIPPIANS 3:20-21 THE MESSAGE

This world is not our home;
we are looking forward to our city
in heaven, which is yet to come.

HEBREWS 13:14 NLT

TREASURE

God made each
of us unique, and there
is a vast mystery and beauty
surrounding the human soul.

ALAN LOY MCGINNIS

"If you will listen obediently to what I say and
keep My covenant, out of all peoples
you'll be My special treasure."

EXODUS 19:5 THE MESSAGE

You made all the delicate, inner parts
of my body and knit me together in my
mother's womb. Thank You for making me so
wonderfully complex! Your workmanship is
marvelous – and how well I know it.

PSALM 139:13-14 NLT

"I would not forget you!
See, I have written your
name on My hand."

ISAIAH 49:15-16 NLT

"They will be Mine," says the
LORD Almighty, "in the day when
I make up My treasured possession.
I will spare them, just as in compassion a man
spares his son who serves him."

MALACHI 3:17

The LORD has declared today that you
are His people, His own special
treasure, just as He promised.

DEUTERONOMY 26:18 NLT

"I have summoned you by name;
you are Mine. You are precious and
honored in My sight, and I love you."

ISAIAH 43:1, 4 NKJV

TRIUMPHANT

One person
with God is always
in the majority.

JOHN KNOX

For the LORD your God is the one who
goes with you to fight for you against
your enemies to give you victory.

DEUTERONOMY 20:4

You give me Your shield of victory;
You stoop down to make me great.

2 SAMUEL 22:36

Every child of God defeats
this evil world by trusting Christ
to give the victory.

1 JOHN 5:4 NLT

He holds victory in store for
the upright, He is a shield to those
whose walk is blameless, for He guards
the course of the just and protects
the way of His faithful ones.

PROVERBS 2:7-8

"I have told you all this so that you may have
peace in Me. Here on earth you will have
many trials and sorrows. But take heart,
because I have overcome the world."

JOHN 16:33 NLT

TRUE-HEARTED

Honesty of thought
and speech and written
word is a jewel, and they
who curb prejudice and seek
honorably to know and speak
the truth are the only builders
of a better life.

JOHN GALSWORTHY

Truthful witness by a good
person clears the air, but liars lay
down a smoke screen of deceit.

PROVERBS 12:17 THE MESSAGE

Keep a close watch on yourself and on your
teaching. Stay true to what is right, and God
will save you and those who hear you.

1 TIMOTHY 4:16 NLT

Who may ascend the hill of the LORD?
Who may stand in His holy place? He who
has clean hands and a pure heart,
who does not swear by what is false.

PSALM 24:3-4

Always keep your conscience clear.
For some people have deliberately
violated their consciences; as a result,
their faith has been shipwrecked.

1 TIMOTHY 1:19 NLT

The truthful lip shall be established forever,
but a lying tongue is but for a moment.

PROVERBS 12:19 NKJV

Trust in the LORD with all your heart
and lean not on your own understanding;
in all your ways acknowledge Him,
and He will make your paths straight.

PROVERBS 3:5-6

TRUSTING

Trust God for great
things; with your five
loaves and two fishes,
He will show you a way
to feed thousands.

HORACE BUSHNELL

Blessed are those who trust
in the LORD and have made the LORD
their hope and confidence.

JEREMIAH 17:7 NLT

Yes, indeed – God is my salvation.
I trust, I won't be afraid.
God – yes God! –
is my strength and song.

ISAIAH 12:2 THE MESSAGE

Things work out when
you trust in God.

PROVERBS 16:20 THE MESSAGE

Trust in Him at all times, O people;
pour out your hearts to Him,
for God is our refuge.

PSALM 62:8

May the God of hope
fill you with all joy and peace
in believing, that you may
abound in hope by the power
of the Holy Spirit.

ROMANS 15:13 NKJV

Trust in the LORD forever,
for the LORD, the LORD,
is the Rock eternal.

ISAIAH 26:4

She watches over the
ways of her household,
and does not eat
the bread of idleness.

PROVERBS 31:27 NKJV

YOU ARE WORTH
far more
THAN
RUBIES

PROVERBS 31:10

A woman of W-O-R-T-**H** is heart-healthy
and heavenly-minded as she strives to
live a holy life. She is forever hopeful and
has a hunger for God and His Word.

HAPPY

Now that I know Christ,
I'm happier when I'm
sad than I was before
when I was glad.

JOHN C. WHEELER

May the righteous be glad
and rejoice before God;
may they be happy and joyful.

PSALM 68:3

Happy are those who have the
God of Israel as their helper,
whose hope is in the LORD their God.

PSALM 146:5 NLT

Happy are those who fear the L<small>ORD</small>.
Yes, happy are those who delight
in doing what He commands.

PSALM 112:1 NLT

A happy heart makes the face cheerful,
but heartache crushes the spirit.

PROVERBS 15:13

I know the L<small>ORD</small> is always with me.
I will not be shaken, for He is right beside me.
No wonder my heart is filled with joy,
and my mouth shouts His praises.

PSALM 16:8-9 NLT

A simple life in the Fear-of-God is
better than a rich life with a ton of headaches.

PROVERBS 15:16 THE MESSAGE

The joy of the L<small>ORD</small> is your strength.

NEHEMIAH 8:10 NLT

HARMONY

Minimize friction
and create harmony.
You can get friction for
nothing, but harmony costs
courage and self-control.

ELBERT HUBBARD

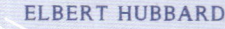

Live in harmony with one another.
Do not be proud, but be willing to
associate with people of low position.
Do not be conceited. If it is possible,
as far as it depends on you,
live at peace with everyone.

ROMANS 12:16, 18

How wonderful, how beautiful,
when brothers and sisters get along!

PSALM 133:1 THE MESSAGE

Finally, all of you, live in harmony
with one another; be sympathetic,
love as brothers, be compassionate
and humble. Do not repay evil with evil
or insult with insult, but with blessing,
because to this you were called so
that you may inherit a blessing.

1 PETER 3:8-9

May God, who gives this patience
and encouragement, help you live in
complete harmony with each other –
each with the attitude of Christ
Jesus toward the other.

ROMANS 15:5 NLT

"May they be brought to complete
unity to let the world know that You
sent Me and have loved them even
as You have loved Me."

JOHN 17:23

HEART-HEALTHY

For Christ is the
God over all, who has
arranged to wash away sin
from mankind, rendering
the old man new.

HIPPOLYTUS

If anyone is in Christ, he is a new creation;
the old has gone, the new has come!

2 CORINTHIANS 5:17

"Though your sins are like scarlet,
they shall be as white as snow;
though they are red like crimson,
they shall be as wool."

ISAIAH 1:18 NKJV

Physical exercise has some value,
but spiritual exercise is much
more important, for it promises a reward
in both this life and the next.

1 TIMOTHY 4:8 NLT

Let us draw near to God with a
sincere heart in full assurance of faith,
having our hearts sprinkled to cleanse us
from a guilty conscience and having our
bodies washed with pure water.

HEBREWS 10:22

Create in me a clean heart, O God,
and renew a steadfast spirit within me.

PSALM 51:10 NKJV

He heals the brokenhearted,
binding up their wounds.

PSALM 147:3 NLT

HEAVENLY-MINDED

Our destination is home with our Father in heaven. It is so easy on this journey to lose sight of our destination. This life is only the trip to get home.

BOB SNYDER

Our citizenship is in heaven.
And we eagerly await a Savior from there,
the Lord Jesus Christ, who, by the power that
enables Him to bring everything under His
control, will transform our lowly bodies so
that they will be like His glorious body.

PHILIPPIANS 3:20-21

We are looking forward to the new
heavens and new earth He has promised,
a world where everyone is right with God.

2 PETER 3:13 NLT

We always pray for you, for we heard
that you trust in Christ Jesus and that
you love all of God's people. You do this
because you are looking forward to the joys
of heaven – as you have been ever since you
first heard the truth of the Good News.

COLOSSIANS 1:3-5 NLT

He has given us new birth into a living
hope through the resurrection of Jesus
Christ from the dead, and into an inheritance
that can never perish, spoil or fade –
kept in heaven for you.

1 PETER 1:3-4

"In My Father's house are many mansions;
if it were not so, I would have told you.
I go to prepare a place for you. And if I go
and prepare a place for you, I will come
again and receive you to Myself."

JOHN 14:2-3 NKJV

HELPMATE

**Be the mate God
designed you to be.**

ANTHONY T. EVANS

The Lord God said, "It is not good that man
should be alone; I will make him a helper
comparable to him." Then the rib which the
Lord God had taken from man He made into a
woman, and He brought her to the man.

GENESIS 2:18, 22 NKJV

Give honor to marriage, and remain
faithful to one another in marriage.
God will surely judge people who are
immoral and those who commit adultery.

HEBREWS 13:4 NLT

"Haven't you read that
the Creator originally made man
and woman for each other,
male and female? And because of this,
a man leaves father and mother
and is firmly bonded to his wife,
becoming one flesh – no longer
two bodies but one."

MATTHEW 19:4-6 THE MESSAGE

The wife God gives you is your
reward for all your earthly toil.

ECCLESIASTES 9:9 NLT

Who can find a virtuous and capable wife?
She is worth more than precious rubies.
Her husband can trust her, and she will
greatly enrich his life. She will not hinder
him but help him all her life.

PROVERBS 31:10-12 NLT

HEROIC

Courage is not
the absence of fear,
but the judgment that
something else is more
important than fear.

AMBROSE REDMOON

"Don't be afraid, for I am with you.
Do not be dismayed, for I am your God.
I will strengthen you. I will help you. I will
uphold you with My victorious right hand."

ISAIAH 41:10 NLT

"Be strong and courageous. Do not be terrified;
do not be discouraged, for the Lord your God
will be with you wherever you go."

JOSHUA 1:9

Commit everything you do to the Lord.
Trust Him, and He will help you.

PSALM 37:5 NLT

The Lord is my light and my salvation;
whom shall I fear? The Lord is the strength of
my life; of whom shall I be afraid?

PSALM 27:1 NKJV

When you go out to battle against
your enemies, do not be afraid of them;
for the Lord your God is with you.

DEUTERONOMY 20:1 NKJV

Be strong in the Lord and
in His mighty power.

EPHESIANS 6:10

HOLY

A holy life
will produce
the deepest impression.
Lighthouses blow no horns;
they only shine.

DWIGHT L. MOODY

As He who called you is holy,
you also be holy in all your conduct,
because it is written, "Be holy, for I am holy."

1 PETER 1:15-16 NKJV

Make every effort to live
in peace with all men
and to be holy; without holiness
no one will see the Lord.

HEBREWS 12:14

Long ago, even before He made the world,
God loved us and chose us in Christ to be holy
and without fault in His eyes.

EPHESIANS 1:4 NLT

I beseech you therefore, by the mercies of
God, that you present your bodies a living
sacrifice, holy, acceptable to God, which is
your reasonable service.

ROMANS 12:1 NKJV

Your sins have been washed away,
and you have been set apart for God.

1 CORINTHIANS 6:11 NLT

Don't you realize that all of you together are
the temple of God and that the Spirit of God
lives in you? God will bring ruin upon anyone
who ruins this temple. For God's temple is
holy, and you Christians are that temple.

1 CORINTHIANS 3:16-17 NLT

HOMEMAKER

This is the true
nature of home – it is the
place of peace, the shelter,
not only from injury,
but from all terror,
doubt, and division.

JOHN RUSKIN

The LORD blesses the
home of the righteous.

PROVERBS 3:33

How happy are those who fear
the LORD. Look at all those children!
There they sit around your table
as vigorous and healthy as
young olive trees.

PSALM 128:1, 3 NLT

Don't you see that children
are God's best gift? The fruit of
the womb His generous legacy?

PSALM 127:3 THE MESSAGE

She rises while it is yet night,
and provides food for her household.
She is not afraid of snow for her household,
for all her household is clothed with scarlet.

PROVERBS 31:15, 21 NKJV

She watches over the ways of her household
and does not eat the bread of idleness.

PROVERBS 31:27 NKJV

By wisdom a house is built, and through
understanding it is established; through
knowledge its rooms are filled with rare and
beautiful treasures.

PROVERBS 24:3-4

HOPEFUL

Behind the cloud the starlight lurks, through showers the sunbeams fall; for God who loveth all His works, has left His hope for all.

JOHN GREENLEAF WHITTIER

May the God of hope fill you with all joy and peace as you trust in Him, so that you may overflow with hope by the power of the Holy Spirit.

ROMANS 15:13

Let us hold fast the confession of our hope without wavering, for He who promised is faithful.

HEBREWS 10:23 NKJV

"I know what I'm doing. I have it all
planned out – plans to take care of you,
not abandon you, plans to give you
the future you hope for."

JEREMIAH 29:11 THE MESSAGE

Hope does not disappoint us, because God
has poured out His love into our hearts by the
Holy Spirit, whom He has given us.

ROMANS 5:5

I wait for the LORD, my soul waits,
and in His word I put my hope.

PSALM 130:5

What is faith? It is the confident assurance
that what we hope for is going to happen.
It is the evidence of things we cannot yet see.

HEBREWS 11:1 NLT

HOSPITALITY

**Hospitality
should have no
other nature than love.**
HENRIETTA C. MEARS

Don't forget to show hospitality
to strangers, for some who have done this
have entertained angels without realizing it!

HEBREWS 13:2 NLT

"When you give a feast, invite the poor,
the maimed, the lame, the blind.
And you will be blessed, because they cannot
repay you; for you shall be repaid
at the resurrection of the just."

LUKE 14:13-14 NKJV

Be quick to give a meal to the hungry,
a bed to the homeless – cheerfully.
Be generous with the different things
God gave you.

1 PETER 4:9-10 THE MESSAGE

A generous man will prosper; he who
refreshes others will himself be refreshed.

PROVERBS 11:25

You will be enriched so that you can
give even more generously. And when we
take your gifts to those who need them,
they will break out in thanksgiving to God.

2 CORINTHIANS 9:11 NLT

Command them to do good,
to be rich in good deeds, and to be generous
and willing to share. In this way they will lay
up treasure for themselves.

1 TIMOTHY 6:18-19

HUMBLE

What makes
humility desirable is
the marvelous thing it does
in us; it creates a capacity
for the closest possible
intimacy with God.

MONICA BALDWIN

The LORD takes pleasure
in His people; He will beautify
the humble with salvation.

PSALM 149:4 NKJV

Humble yourselves in the sight
of the Lord, and He will lift you up.

JAMES 4:10 NKJV

Be content with who you are,
and don't put on airs.
God's strong hand is on you;
He'll promote you at the right time.

1 PETER 5:6-7 THE MESSAGE

"For whoever exalts himself
will be humbled, and whoever
humbles himself will be exalted."

MATTHEW 23:12

Those who are gentle and lowly
will posses the land; they will live
in prosperous security.

PSALM 37:11 NLT

Pride leads to disgrace,
but with humility comes wisdom.

PROVERBS 11:2 NLT

HUNGER FOR GOD

You called, You cried,
You shattered my deafness:
You flashed, You shone,
You scattered my blindness:
You breathed fragrance,
and I drew in my breath,
and I pant for You!

ST. AUGUSTINE

Oh, how I love Your law!
I meditate on it all day long.
How sweet are Your words to my taste,
sweeter than honey to my mouth!

PSALM 119:97, 103

God proves to be good to the
man who passionately waits,
to the woman who diligently seeks.

LAMENTATIONS 3:25 THE MESSAGE

"Ask, and it will be given to you;
seek, and you will find; knock, and it will
be opened to you. For everyone who asks
receives, and he who seeks finds, and to him
who knocks it will be opened."

MATTHEW 7:7-8 NKJV

He satisfies the thirsty and
fills the hungry with good things.

PSALM 107:9

If you search for Him with all your
heart and soul, you will find Him.

DEUTERONOMY 4:29 NLT

I am fearfully and wonderfully made.

PSALM 139:14

As the deer pants for streams of water,
so my soul pants for You, O God.
My soul thirsts for God, for the living God.

PSALM 42:1-2

O God, You are my God,
earnestly I seek You;
my soul thirsts for You.

PSALM 63:1